PARENTING without a Paddle

Navigating the Waters of Parenthood

PARENTING without a Paddle

Navigating the Waters of Parenthood

An Inspirational Parenting Guide

Kristin Fitch

Sharon Pierce McCullough

ZiggityZoom

Published by
Ziggity Zoom
www.ZiggityZoom.com

www.ParentingWithoutaPaddle.com

ISBN-13:978-0-9831915-0-6

ISBN-10:0-9831915-0-6

Printed in the United States of America.

First Printing: January 2011

Library of Congress Cataloging-in-Publication Data
is available from the publisher.

Cover Illustration : iStock Photo/ Nahhan

For

*All my Children and Grandchildren who I am thankful
for each and every day.   SPMc*

For

The Lord above who has given me so much.

*My mom, my co-author, who amazes me every single
day with her love, kindness, patience, drive and
creativity. The world is a happier place because of her.*

My husband Trip- for always loving and supporting me.

*My kids- for your hugs, smiles, and the lessons you
teach me every day.*

*My sister, Kira- for your kind heart, gentle ways and
God given talents.*

*My brothers, Chris, Randy, and Ryan- you are kind,
giving, funny, and supportive.*

*My dad- for showing me how to embrace life and
always make it an adventure.*

*My entire family of relatives- Pierces, Millers, Fitches,
Brashes– each one of you inspire me. I have never
met another family like ours. We are blessed to have
each other. I have seen love, kindness, inspiration,
and support through every one of you. – KF*

Contents

You Can Never Say "I Love You" Too Much

Thankfulness

Meditation & Prayer

Teach Kindness by Example

Introduction

Inspire Love, Hope, Kindness, Laughter

Making the decision to have a child is momentous. It is to decide forever to have your heart go walking around outside your body.

Elizabeth Stone

Welcome to the greatest adventure of your life, Parenthood. Being a parent is one of the most fulfilling experiences you will ever have. It brings great joy and love into your life, but it will also take you on a roller coaster ride like no other experience. There will be ups and downs and unexpected turns. As a parent you will even find yourself upside down without knowing which way is up. Parenting is a special opportunity for you to nurture one of life's greatest creations, a child, and to guide them into becoming a beautiful human being. There will be great successes while you raise your child and often there will be great hurdles you will have to conquer, but the payoff is huge. You will develop an amazing relationship with a person you have helped to shape. Parenting does not stop when your child is old enough to live on her own. Parenting continues throughout your child's life, even when your child becomes an adult.

No Instruction Manual

Having children makes you no more a parent than having a piano makes you a pianist.

Michael Levine

As a parent you have made or will make great preparations for the arrival of your child. You get the room ready, with a crib, diapers, clothes, blankets, wipes, pacifiers, and all the things a baby could need or want.

The big day arrives. You take your precious child home and that's when it first hits you. There is NO instruction manual ... None ... NADA. Actually, I think I first realized this little detail while still in the hospital with my first born. I had absolutely no clue what to do with a baby. Sure, I had taken a few prenatal classes, but I had never been around many babies or small children.

In nature, animals recognize their babies by smell or sound. Seal mothers go hunting, and, when they return mother and baby easily find one another. I'm sorry, but when my babies were first born, if you had put a bunch of babies in a room, I don't think I could have picked out my own baby, especially if others were similar in size and hair color.

So. No manual, no homing instinct. What's a parent to do? Wing it. That is what all parents do. Why? Because every child is different. Every day is different. The possibilities are endless. Yes, you may follow some of the same direction that your parents took regarding parenting, but, obviously, you will have no recollections about how your parents handled situations when you were very young.

Whether you are near the beginning of your parenting journey, the middle or in the final stretch, all parents need to keep in mind that parenting is definitely one of the most difficult jobs on earth, but it can also be the most rewarding.

Even though there is no instruction booklet, you, as a parent, do have inner resources to pull from. These are your parenting tools. You will hone these tools on a daily basis, and your parenting skills will improve and develop as you grow with your child. A key point to remember is that each child is uniquely different, and the parenting technique you develop with one child may not work with another.

What **inner resources** will help you to develop good parenting skills?

Love. This is the basis of your parent-child relationship. Without love, no one will have much of a chance to succeed as a good parent.

Patience. While some parents have an abundance of this virtue, many of us have to work hard on this. We all falter at times, but this is a key ingredient to good parenting.

Kindness. Essential to raising a kind child is your own kindness. Even discipline should be enacted with kindness.

Honesty. Being truthful to your children will help them to be honest themselves. Teach truthfulness by your own example.

Discipline. One of the hardest parts of parenting is learning to properly and kindly discipline your child. We must also discipline ourselves, learning to use restraint in our own lives, as well as when dealing with our children.

Acceptance. Key to building self-esteem in a child is acceptance. Positive words and actions go a long way in displaying our acceptance of our children.

Humor. Another essential ingredient to good parenting is humor, the use of which helps foster happiness. Learn to laugh and laugh often.

It takes a Village

It's not only children who grow. Parents do too. As much as we watch to see what our children do with their lives, they are watching us to see what we do with ours. I can't tell my children to reach for the sun. All I can do is reach for it, myself.

Joyce Maynard

While raising my five children, I was not fortunate to have family close by. It was often difficult plus I had a husband who was in the Navy and out to sea often. But, regardless of your own personal situation, reach out and ask for help when you truly need it. Remember that asking for help is not a weakness.

Ask any child you know how often they have to get help from someone. They probably can't count the many times a day they ask a parent, teacher, caregiver, or sibling to help them. Just because we grow up and become a parent doesn't mean we should be able to do it all.

Know that you will need help raising your child. Some of us might need help daily, getting a break from our children to re-energize. Others may need help when there is a scheduling conflict or if someone becomes ill. You may need unlimited support if you have child with special needs or have multiples. A supportive spouse is a godsend when raising your child if you are in a marriage.

Do not hesitate to ask other parents for assistance in setting up systems such as organized playdates or a carpool. All of these types of things are good support systems that help both you and the other parents involved.

Immediate family, neighbors, and friends are life savers when you are raising children. Don't be afraid to ask for help if you are feeling overwhelmed or an emergency arises. And if you are lucky enough to live close to grandparents, involve them in your children's daily lives. It will enhance your child's life and theirs. It will also make life a little bit easier for you as a parent.

Reminders:

- Don't go it alone.

- Ask for help when you need it.

- Allow yourself short periods of alone time, when possible.

Use Your Instincts

Too often we underestimate the power of a touch, a smile, a kind word, a listening ear, an honest compliment, or the smallest act of caring, all of which have the potential to turn a life around.

Leo Buscaglia

A key thought to keep in mind is that most of us have pretty good instincts. As long as we use good common sense and our moral compass, we will do just fine raising our children.

Our main goal, in writing this book, is to help support you as a parent and provide resources, helpful suggestions, and information learned from experience. Believe me, in parenting, experience is invaluable! So keep in mind that you do have the basics wired inside of you to do a good job parenting. As with all things in life, it is helpful to have a good support system.

Make a List of your already acquired attributes that you think will help you in parenting.

- Are you a good listener?

- Are you patient?

- Are you a good leader?

- Can you find humor in situations?

- Do you have a positive outlook?

- Do you accept help when it is offered?

Big Dose of Laughter

Humor makes all things tolerable.

Henry Ward Beecher

I have heard that children laugh 10,000 times in a week and adults only laugh 10 times. I figure if I am fortunate enough to spend time with my kids, I will be one of the lucky ones to laugh often.

If there is one thing I would suggest to make parenting easier, it would be to learn to laugh more. There are many days and many nights that you might just feel like crying. If you can learn to laugh at situations, even little things that happen that seem overwhelming, you will be happier. Your child will be happier, your spouse will be happier, and you will have deflected some stress from yourself.

I believe, as parents, we have a big lesson to learn here. Happiness and humor so have a place, or should, in our daily lives. As the saying goes "Laughter is the best medicine" … have a little each day.

Our Advice:

- Learn to Laugh often.

- Be open to the Joys of Parenting.

- Be able to laugh at yourself.

- Ask for Help when you need it.

- Being present, not perfect, is what matters.

Pushing Off without a Paddle

Allow children to be happy their own way; for what better way will they find?

Samuel Johnson

Once you've gotten your toes wet, you just have to jump right in ... life vest or not. Once your child is born, there is no turning back. You are now the protector, the parent.

I know, I know, some parents make it seem so easy, almost effortless ... Well, let me tell you, some kids are just born as the "model child" ... period. They never cry, whine, or get into a hissy fit. You would swear they were little pleasant robots, they are that perfect. And I must admit ... I did have one child, out of five, that was Mr. Happy, Smiley all the time. But I never had a baby, like some moms I know, who stayed in his crib until late in the mornings, cooing and just waiting for mom to arrive. No, everyone of my kids woke at 6:00 or 6:30 in the morning hungry and wanting to be fed right away.

Your primary job as a parent, besides caring for your child's needs, is that of a teacher. And even though you may not think of yourself as a teacher, here are some of the subtle, and not so subtle, things your child will be learning from you.

- **How to treat people**

- **How to interact with people**

- **What is really important in life**

Your child should learn the most basic and important elements of being a good human being from you, as parent, and your examples. We are not all born with eloquence when it comes to talking to our children, but honesty and providing a good example do prevail. This I know from experience. By our example, our children will learn respect of others, social interaction skills, listening skills and good sportsmanship. They will learn priorities, such as faith, family, and self.

Everything you do, everything you say, and how you respond to situations will affect the way your child develops as an individual. You, more than anyone else, will help shape your child into who he becomes.

Exercise:

Think of the people you admire most in this world. Which qualities do you admire the most in them? Make a mental note that these are the qualities that you have the ability to help develop in your own child. As a reminder, jot down your list and look at it occasionally.

Destination Unknown

Life is what happens to you while you're busy making other plans.

John Lennon

No one has a crystal ball and often, even when you have a mapped-out plan, things change. Life just happens and sometimes you feel as though you are in a maze. As a parent, it is necessary to develop a sense of flexibility. If you can be flexible, you will reduce the stress around you and your family. Routine and structure are vitally important but, as a parent, you need to be adaptable.

One of my biggest accomplishments, as a parent, has been to accept spur of the moment changes. I am, now, consistently flexible, even though I wasn't originally so. You know the saying "Don't sweat the small things." It is so important to remember. When something disrupts your day, week, or life, try to take a moment and put it into perspective. How important is it really?

Reminders:

- Keep things in perspective.
- Be optimistic.
- Be flexible.

- Be thankful.

Tour Guide

If you don't paddle your own canoe you don't move.

Katharine Hepburn

There are two types of tour guides. The first is a guide that does tours because that is his job. This tour guide just goes through the motions without much thought. It is his job. It is what is expected of him. The second tour guide loves his job. He loves sharing with everyone what he knows. Both tour guides wear similar outfits, and much of what they say is the same. Yet the experience visitors get from the two tours is quite different.

The first group quickly grows disinterested, and the group begins talking among themselves. That same group asks very few questions, and there is minimal excitement from the group.

The second group's experience is much different. The guide shares extra facts and caters the tour to the group's interests and purpose for taking the tour. This group asks tons of questions and wants to return again for another guided tour. Their experience has been enhanced by the enthusiastic, prepared, and engaging tour guide.

Parenting is much the same. There are parents who are present in their children's lives yet they are only going through the motions. They feed, bathe, and provide their children with the basics and even sign them up for classes, arrange activities and play dates. These parents love their children, but they may be so overworked, stressed, or stretched too thin, that they do not even realize they are missing an important element, that of sharing real joy, participating with and teaching their children with passion.

The second group of parents shows their kids about the joys of life, nurtures them and teaches them with a passion. For these parents, parenting is not a job, another thing to fit in every day, for them it is their passion and love that comes through. The first group of parents loves their children, but they let the burdens of life and stress, or exhaustion, dictate how they parent. We encourage parents to parent with passion and happiness. This will help their children grow and become independent, confident adults one day. How do parents do this when the demands on them can be so great?

Be the tour guide for them who instills excitement for life and for the things you are passionate about. Allow them to ask questions, even the uncomfortable ones, and answer them honestly. Allow your children to be part of the process of life. If you cook, allow your children to help you- let them be creative with it- even if it takes longer or they don't do it your way. Let them find their passions in life by trying out new things and learning about the world around them. Be a rock star tour guide for your kids.

Parenting Tips:

- Talk to kids about things/subjects that interest you.

- Ask your kids what interests them.

- Foster a desire to learn.

- Explore your world as a family.

Stop, Look, Listen

Believe you can and you're halfway there.

Theodore Roosevelt

Your role is akin to a guide even though you have no map and your destination is unknown. The waters of parenthood are filled with unseen obstacles. But you can navigate these waters using good common sense.

Be present. This is one of the foremost requirements of being a good parent. It's easy enough to tune out the kids, over-stay at work, or stay involved in your own pursuits. But that is not good parenting. Sometimes, for sanity's sake, we do need to tune out, but this shouldn't be the norm.

Kids need to feel wanted and loved, and it is imperative if you are trying to raise a well-rounded and emotionally healthy child. Assess each situation during your parenting day willingly, rather than begrudgingly. It's an easy trap to fall into. Even if you're feeling slightly overwhelmed, remember to keep these little rules in mind.

Parenting Rules of Navigation:

- **Stop**   Don't panic. Relax. Breathe.

- **Look**   Assess the situation.

- **Listen**   Think, listen and respond to situations as calmly as possible. If you respond to situations in a highly stressed manner, kids will respond exactly the same. Be calm, but assertive.

Great Expectations

Children are apt to live up to what you believe of them.

Lady Bird Johnson

We all have certain expectations when entering parenthood. But regardless of those expectations, there are basic concepts that we all need to follow in order to raise children who are happy with themselves for who they are as individuals.

How you treat and react to your children will have an absolute effect on their self-esteem and self-image. Take every opportunity to let your children know that they are innately good. You can let them know that you don't approve of certain actions, but that you, nonetheless, still love them for who they are.

If a parent constantly reinforces that a child is "bad" or misbehaves all the time, then that is exactly what you will get in return ... more bad behavior. They will see no reason to be good because you are expecting them to be bad. You have actually told them so. So, do expect goodness and you will be rewarded with better behavior. This isn't always an easy thing to do, but it will work.

Parents need to practice what they preach. Look for a career or hobby you love and go for it. Find time to spend with your family when you can fully engage and connect. Get out of your comfort zone and plunge, feet first, into a new experience with your kids. Show your children how to love by showing them how much you love them, and others, with loving words, gestures, and giving them yourself and your time.

Our Advice:

- Even though we do not start out with the tools and knowledge for parenting, we will gather all the information we need along the way and develop new skills ourselves.

- Remember that you are dealing with a child and try to keep the age of the child in perspective to your expectations.

- Don't let yourself be the one "behaving badly".

Adventures of a Lifetime

Each child is an adventure into a better life - an opportunity to change the old pattern and make it new.

Hubert H. Humphrey

Parenting is a lifelong trip down obscure roads, up steep mountains, and down into valleys. It is a joyful trip filled with laughter and smiles. There are twists and turns, but your child's smile can melt your heart, turn a bad day into a good day, and an "I love you" can positively light up the world for you.

If we are to teach our children to become responsible adults who give back to the world by giving of themselves and their talents and abilities, we must first be an example to them of someone who gives to the world what we can. If we, as parents, are fortunate enough to find something to be passionate about, and we pursue it, our example will have shown them the possibility for them to do the same.

Life with kids is a true adventure in every sense of the word. There is nothing more exciting than watching your own child make new discoveries, new friends, and new observations. Be open to these opportunities as the moments pass too quickly.

Step in and share as many "firsts" with your child as possible. It will be rewarding to both of you and not easily forgotten.

Remember:

- You are your child's primary example. Inspire him.

- Life is what you make it. Make it an adventure.

- Be open to new thoughts, new places, and new friends.

Enjoy the Ride

Dream as if you'll live forever. Live as if you'll die tomorrow.

James Dean

A road trip is an exciting time for a family as family members pile in a car and head towards their vacation destination. Yet the road trip itself is often the part of the trip that allows a family to connect and make memories that will last a lifetime. What other times do you have hours to spend together without going in five different directions? Sure there are electronics and DVD players in cars today, but that does not mean you should allow an entire trip to pass without taking some time to connect as a family. Limit the number of movies, or music, kids can watch or listen to in the car. Allow times during the drive so that you can play games together or ask questions or even sing songs. This might sound corny, and some kids will be against this, but secretly most like it.

The road to get to our destination is often the time when learning or bonding experiences happen. I took a trip recently with one of my brothers, my mom, and my dad. (My brother and I are grown now and have our own families, and my parents are both remarried.) We were going to my sister's wedding in Nicaragua for a quick weekend. We happened to have brought along a dice game and played that game for hours during airport layovers. We had a great time, enjoyed each other's company, and it relaxed everyone. It is amazing how something as simple as a game can affect an entire group of people. In a car you can play I Spy, Letter Search, Colored Cars, and so many other games. It is about making it fun for your family. Take a brief pit stop or detour and check out some strange, or interesting, tourist sites. When we were on a road trip to a Safari Park with the kids, we dined at the Pink Diner. It was not the type of restaurant I normally would have picked but it was pink, but the building was pink, there was a King Kong statue in front, and the décor inside has a rock n' roll theme. It was a place we will remember because it was different from hitting the nearest fast-food joint.

Bring Along Your Camera

The future belongs to those who believe in the beauty of their dreams.

Bart Forbes

There is no better way to capture a lazy day, a vacation, or a special occasion than with a picture or journal entry. Often, as parents, it is so easy to get caught up in the details of a birthday, vacation, or even a busy day that we forget about each little blessing, tidbit of love and wisdom that is passed back and forth between our children and us each and every day. We may be over worked, lacking sleep, or have too many demands on us, but when we capture the moments and capture our children's smiles, it is a magical moment that has been preserved. When we step back and observe the moment and our child's face, we will see the love and happiness of our children right in front of us. Often we miss joy in the everyday moment and encounters. Your children will appreciate the snapshots you took of them and the family as they get older and continue to look at the photos.

Even looking at a photo of your child at a later date will make you happy that you captured their spirit. Just reminiscing while looking through old photos of your children can be a relaxing, stress-relieving activity.

One note: make sure you take pictures/videos of all of your kids. Often, if a family has multiple kids, it can get more difficult as time passes to capture the special moments and occasions with a camera, and your younger kids may have very few pictures of themselves as children. I know because this happened to me, and I am very purposeful about taking lots of pictures of all of my kids.

Build a Fort

It is a happy talent to know how to play.

Ralph Waldo Emerson

Can you remember being a child? Do you ever remember climbing a tree or making a fort? Or do you remember pretending to be a cowboy or Indian? Your imagination was limitless. The sky could be purple and the grass blue. The world could be filled with lollipops and candy canes or anything else you imagined.

Children love forts, tree houses and hiding spots. Forts might mess up the living room when your kids use all of the cushions or sheets to make a fort, but, remember, for kids it isn't as much about the fort as the amazing places they can go, things they can imagine, and adventurers they can have in their fort. They are pretending. And guess what? Pretending is an important part of being a kid. It's actually a very healthy and necessary part of childhood. It allows children to be creative, come up with solutions, and role-play.

Our advice: Pull out the sheets and make a fort with your kids. If you're lucky, they might even invite you in if you can summon up a creative character or spell binding story. Maybe you can even muster up the energy to build a tree house or fort out back for your kids. But remember what is most important is allowing your kids to pretend and be silly and explore the world of real and make-believe from the safety of their home. So encourage building forts and silly creatures, characters and things from real life and made-up stories from when you were a child.

Dig Deep

Your children vividly remember every unkind thing you ever did to them, plus a few you really didn't.

Mignon McLaughlin

Big Adventures call for some pretty big efforts, and parenting is a very big adventure that lasts a lifetime. It is difficult to prepare for such a long adventure, but some knowledge and advice will help you get through the adventure.

Patience and Kindness are two necessary qualities parents need, yet they are qualities that do not come easily for many people. Learning to stay calm when your baby is screaming with colic for hours, or when your teenager refuses to do anything you say, will challenge most of us, it will test our patience and ability to stay calm, but we have to remember that we are in control. We must stay calm in order to lead and handle any situation that occurs.

I worked for a newspaper company for years, and one thing I took away from the job was a saying about how one should act as if it applies to all facets of our life. I believe if we considered our actions and words in this context, more of us would act better more often.

Make sure that whatever you do, or whatever you say, you would be all right having it printed on the front page of your newspaper. In other words, if you say or do things that you would be embarrassed for others to know about or that could land you in trouble, then assume you should not be saying or doing them in the first place. Another way to put it is, if everything you did and said was recorded for your parents, siblings, friends, co-workers and neighbors to see, would you have cursed or screamed at your kid or given them a swat? Be guided by your own moral compass and your own understanding of right and wrong and what is appropriate and inappropriate, kind and unkind behavior. Let this compass guide your actions and words with your kids. And for those parents that need even more reason to keep your cool and stay calm with your kids, think about having your face and actions or words land on the front page of your newspaper or favorite news site.

Suggestions:

Always have a Plan B. One option for Plan B is to leave the room for five minutes before even speaking if an episode is driving your emotions out of control. This is preferable to shouting out words or phrases for which you may later be sorry. Don't let anyone, or any event, take control of your emotions.

Hidden Treasure

Happiness is a direction, not a place.

Sydney J. Harris

You're a parent. You are destined to make mistakes no matter how much you prepare or try to get it perfect as a parent. The mistakes will not define your parenting, but the way you parent the rest of the time and the way you handle the mistakes will.

Your job is to realize the journey of raising a child into adulthood is the gem you have been given. A treasure is often something that has a defined value and is usually an inanimate object. But a child will show you a treasure greater than any other, an unconditional love and bond you will have with him/her for your lifetime. The relationship and bond may change over the years, but if you nurture your child, you will continue to uncover new depths and dimensions of the treasure. This treasure lives in your heart and will stay there forever.

When life is going smoothly, it is easy to take a moment and appreciate your child. But when there are ups and downs, or bad behavior crops up, your outlook can quickly be obstructed. Try to always keep things in perspective. Tell your child often how much you treasure him.

Daily Reminders:

- Keep a positive outlook

- Remind yourself of one good thing your child did today.

- Tell your child how much you appreciate the goodness you see in him/her.

Welcome to the Jungle

Have the courage to be yourself.

Fitzhugh Dodson

We have to admit it. Raising a family, even just one child, can get a little wild at times. What parent hasn't experienced days when it seems like a tribe of natives is running around the house? This is especially true if boys are involved.

Having raised both boys and girls, it is almost a given that you will have a rowdier household when boys are living in your house. But regardless of gender, kids can and do get a little crazy at times. Unless it is out of hand, sometimes the best thing to do is join in.

For example, if there's a "pot and pan" parade going through the house ... join in. Your kids will be overjoyed that you have and then if things get a little out of hand, you are now part of the "cause" and can more easily defuse the situation, possibly even with some laughter involved.

Suggestions:

- Participate when possible.

- Have fun with your kids.

- Find ways kids can creatively expend their energy.

Don't Be Afraid to Break All the Rules

Shall we make a new rule of life from tonight?
Always to try to be a little kinder than is necessary.

James M. Barrie

One rule to remember throughout parenthood is that NO two days are ever the same. Just when you think you've gotten a routine going, your child gets sick. Little Mr. Perfect starts acting like Mr. Jeckyl, or the school calls to say your kid has lice.

So any rules you've made often have to be broken ... by you. My kids usually had set bedtimes during the school year, but I recall many times when one of the kids had to stay up late because of extra homework or "last minute" projects. The rules were bent, and life moved on.

It's easier, of course, if the parent is the one breaking her own rules. But be sure to explain to your child exactly why you have chosen to do so or a precedent will have been set, and there may be confusion later.

But what if you have a child who constantly challenges you and has a hard time following household rules? How should you deal with situations like this?

A few suggestions:

- Stay calm

- Assess the situation, remembering to put it into perspective. Take into account whether the child always seems to disobey, and disregard boundaries, or is this a rare occasion?

- Talk to your child and ask him what he would do if he were the parent. This initiates a discussion and makes the child think about his actions and the consequences. Surprisingly, sometimes a child will suggest a stricter time-out or punishment than a parent would give.

- Determine if the misbehavior warrants a warning, a time-out, or a restriction, always trying to be fair.

No question, parenting is one of the most difficult jobs you will ever encounter and probably the most important. Be willing to give it your all and to think outside of the box.

Expect the Unexpected

Opportunities are often right in front of us, but we must recognize them and have the willingness to open the door of possibilities.

Kristin Pierce Fitch

Just when you think you've gotten a handle on things and you even have a routine going, expect the unexpected.

I would say that one of the most important qualities you can develop as a parent is being flexible. Whether you have a newborn or a teenager, there are constantly changing circumstances that require flexibility. Add some humor to that flexibility and you're on the right track.

As the saying goes, "life is what happens while you're making plans." I discovered early in child-rearing that, as a parent, you need to be able to go with the flow. Any parent who is trying to rigidly stick to a routine or plan will be often disappointed. Absolutely, make plans, but plan to be flexible. You will be happier if you can develop a "flexible" mindset.

Questions to ask yourself:

- Am I too rigid in my expectations of my child?

- Could I be a little more flexible when a stressful situation arises?

- Am I remembering to treat my child with respect?

Teachable Moments

While we try to teach our children all about life,
Our children teach us what life is all about.

Angela Schwindt

Often, when a parent focuses on the routine, schedule, rules, and stress of the day, many opportunities to teach our kids or to encourage them are lost. We must be on the look out for teachable moments or opportunities to encourage our children.

The first step is to determine what the things are that we want to be teaching our kids. For instance, you may want to reinforce your religious beliefs, to emphasize treating all humans fairly, or to encourage art, music, and/or reading. If we are not careful, we can miss opportunities to encourage and nurture the things we want to reinforce to our children.

For example, my son was rolling marbles down the stairs and my husband walked by and saw marbles flying down the steps. He believed my son was throwing them down the steps at our other son, and he immediately sent him to time out and disciplined him. I could hear words between them escalating so I went to see what was going on. By this time my husband had gone downstairs. My son said he was not throwing marbles but instead had wanted to see what would happen when the marbles rolled down the steps. I immediately thought of the opportunity to teach about gravity and cause and effect. (No, I am not a science or math person). So I talked to my son about what had happened, had him talk to his dad and apologize for talking back, and we went to find a constructive way he could use marbles, gravity, and his curiosity to play and learn. Two postal tubes, 3 clear containers, and a bowl full of marbles later and my son was off to try out different experiments to make his marbles go down the stairs. It kept him occupied for over an hour.

Another time after putting our kids to bed, my oldest son, who was seven at the time, continued to come out of his room throughout the evening. I continued to tell him to go back to bed and go to sleep. My frustration was getting the best of me. It was getting late, and I had lots to still get done that evening. I snapped at my son when he came into my room the next time, and I told him not to come out of his room again. I had allowed myself to get upset. After I cooled down, I went into his room to tell him I was sorry for being upset with him, but that he did need to get to bed.

Within a matter of minutes he appeared in my room again, and he asked to snuggle with me. I wanted to yell at him to get in bed. I was frustrated with him. Fortunately, I realized his need to be with me was greater than my need to follow a routine or to be in total control. I told him he could come in my room for ten minutes. I compromised by allowing him to come in but also by limiting the time he could stay. As my son snuggled close to me, he shared what had happened at school that day. Someone had taunted him. If I had not let my defenses down and decided to change course, I may have missed hearing about his day and missed the opportunity to give him guidance and reassurance.

Sometimes teachable moments are hidden in challenging, frustrating, or ill-timed situations when we are not feeling very flexible. Try to be more aware of what is going on with your child. If your child takes a while to open up, try to be in tune with his/her communication style. Be aware when your child acts differently, and consider that he/she may need something important from you: love, affection, a private talk, etc.

Teachable moments are not only about the opportunities we use to teach a lesson, make an example out of a particular situation or show our child something. Often teachable moments are brought about by your child when he/she inquires about a topic, idea, or concern. My son asked me the other day if there were five states of matter. He said at school he had heard someone say that, but the science book only mentioned three states of matter. I immediately took this as an opportunity to help my son learn about this new topic that had peaked his interest. When we are so absorbed in our own activities, we can often lose such opportunities to teach our children. Remember to be present, be available, be open and flexible.

Ask Yourself:

- What values do I want to instill in my child?

- Am I a good listener when my child speaks?

- Does my child think I am a good listener?

House of Cards

What's done to children, they will do to society.

Karl Menninger

Imagine a House of Cards ... one wrong move and the house comes falling down. Parenting is much like a house of cards. You work gradually and thoughtfully to build something up, either a house or a child. Each action, conversation, example each day builds your child into the person he/she is today. When we make parenting mistakes or take wrong turns with our children, the house becomes temporarily weaker and might even tumble down. But we can build the house stronger with more cards, or in the case of a child, with more right moves, actions, examples, and words than with wrong ones. As a parent, you are going to make mistakes or not handle every parenting dilemma perfectly. However, over time, you will learn better skills and will have other opportunities to correct past errors or improve upon a poor parenting choice.

It is easy to allow our emotions to control a situation with our child, but we need to remember that each opportunity we have to interact with our child is another opportunity to build our child up in confidence, ability, independence, and love, instead of breaking him/her down. It is so easy for a parent to unknowingly remove a card or just a tiny bit of confidence, love, or strength from a child without even knowing it. We have to focus on how we can build our child up to be the best person possible and to help shape his/her life in a positive manner.

There are times in all parents' lives when you feel that your child is no longer responding to you, and it feels as though all your parenting efforts are tumbling down. This can happen at age three or thirteen or anywhere along the journey. This may be exhibited as defiance, rebellion, or ignoring everything that you say.

If it happens at age three, you feel better equipped to deal with this assertion of independence, and often a talk on your child's level will help you both through this period. Let your child know that you are the parent and you are in charge; however, you have noticed that he wants to do some things of his own choosing. Discuss some of the things that he/she will get to decide on that will be their very own decisions. Now is a perfect time to start letting a child learn about decisions and consequences. Start by letting the child decide what clothes he will wear in the morning. Tell your child what the weather will be each morning and discuss whether shorts and short-sleeved shirt are appropriate. Then let him wear whatever he chooses. Give your child choices. Would he rather have cereal or toast for breakfast? These small things will give your child a feeling of having some control over his own life in minor ways that are acceptable to you as the parent.

When a child is older, often rebellion and defiance relates to a similar display of independence. Many times I have seen parents struggle with this very issue, and it was so obvious that it was a power struggle on both sides. Some parents don't seem to notice that they continue to "issue too many orders" as their child matures. My own way of handling these situations was to remember a few very **simple rules.**

1. Be respectful. Just as children need to respect parents, other adults, and rules, parents need to respect their children.

2. Treat your child with patience, kindness and consistency. Be the parent and stay in charge, but treat your child, and talk to your child with patience and kindness. Be consistent with discipline.

3. Listen to what your child has to say. Too often parents have their own agenda and don't take the time to really listen. This is a common complaint of adolescents. Make the effort to look at your child and pay attention to what he is saying.

4. Try not to give orders. Just as you would ask a friend to do something ... you wouldn't order them ... try to make requests of your child, letting them know your expectations. Children definitely need to obey their parents, but parents can be firm, get obedience, and respect without shouting, and issuing orders.

5.   Exhibit kindness in your words and actions. Treat your child as you would have them treat you, with kindness.

6.   Set House Rules. Setting house rules and following through with consequences when the rules are broken will give your child a secure foundation. Kids need to know the rules and expectations, otherwise there will be chaos.

7.   **Be a protector**.   The safety of our children is a parental responsibility. Let your children know that certain rules are for their own safety and that while they are in your care, their safety is your concern.

This might sound too simple, but it's not. I think you will be amazed at the results if you keep these things in mind when dealing with your child, especially when they are nearing their teen years and beyond.

On occasion, you, as a parent, may be faced with a child who is extremely rebellious. At times like this, you may even have to consider taking away things that the child considers his in order to assert your parental authority. For behavioral difficulties we recommend specific books by experts at the end of this book.

If you do have a child whose rebellion or disobedience continues, and you are unable to get him/her to follow house rules, obey you and straighten up, you need to consider how the current conditions may be allowing them to keep the power. When, in reality, you are the one who needs to take back control of the situation. For instance, in the book The Defiant Child: A Parent's Guide to Oppositional Defiant Disorder by Douglas Riley, he explains that if no other measures to get kids to behave at home and school work, you must consider taking away privileges and anything they value that is not a necessity, such as computer, cell phone, music, special clothing, their bedroom door. In other words, while your children are living in your house, as a minor, you need to provide them with the basics of food, clothing, shelter, but you can remove items that they consider to be theirs in order to establish control and get them to behave. Even though the book is written regarding children and teens with Oppositional Defiant Disorder we feel it is a great strategy to keep in mind when dealing with long term rebellion. We would also mention, that if your child is lashing out, rebelling, depressed, or other major changes occur you should consider seeking professional evaluation or help.

Play and Learn

You can discover more about a person in an hour of play than in a year of conversation.

Plato

Consider a pick-up sports game as kids or men play a game of soccer together. How a player responds to his opponents and teammates can say much about his character. Does he play fairly and follow the rules? Is he polite to his opponents? Or is he mean, unfair and does he cheat? How he behaves greatly reflects how he has been taught since childhood.

Children are constantly learning, from the time they are born. They learn how to get what they need, how to interact with others, how to treat others, how to do things for themselves, all the while developing their character. Kids learn from every experience they have. Whether they are learning manners at the dinner table, how you treat others, even the correct language to use, you are their prime example.

What is interesting is that kids are even learning as they play. And kids play all of the time. Play time is more than having fun, it is a time of learning for children. They will act out what they have observed, things they imagine, and how to interact with others through sharing, playing a game, or through pretend characters.

Our Advice:

- Play with your kids whenever possible.

- Schedule time for yourself, on occasions, to have fun with your spouse or a friend.

- Try to inject fun into mundane routines.

Make Time for Play

Life isn't a matter of milestones but of moments.

Rose Fitzgerald Kennedy

Making time for play is such an important part of your child's growth and development. Kids need free time to play. You do not want to over-schedule your children or they will be exhausted and will not have time to unwind and relax.

When your child plays, he learns to think creatively, work through the events of his life, and work on problem-solving. You will often see a young child playing with little figures or trying to build a structure with blocks; they are actually trying to figure out how things work.

Kids are also working on building social skills.

As your kids get older, they will still play (or now "hang out".) They will play video games with friends or go out and play ball.

It is also important as parents to make time to play with your kids. Children remember a parent playing with them. Whether it is throwing a football outside or playing a board game, kids will keep this memory, and, hopefully, replay the scenario with their children when they grow up and have a family.

You need to get down to a child's level and find an activity that you can both do together. It may take a few times of playing together for you both to enjoy it and have fun. Make sure you disconnect from everything else in your life like work, cell phones, email and focus on spending quality time with your kids.

Even the American Academy of Pediatrics has reported on the topic of play as being crucial to a child's overall development of their imagination, cognitive, physical and creative areas.

Parenting Exercise:

- Schedule "play time" with your child weekly.

- If you have several children, do your best to spend some one-on-one playing time doing something they enjoy.

Learning is Fun

No man is a failure who is enjoying life.

William Feather

Games can teach your children so make learning fun. Use opportunities like dinnertime or driving in the car, or when you are just hanging around the house to use a fun game to bring your family together and teach your kids at the same time.

We enjoy playing a game called "What Else?" We pick an ordinary object to pass around and ask, "What else could this be used for?" or "What else could this be made into?" It is a great way to encourage creative thinking and family togetherness.

You might also enjoy Twenty Questions, I Spy or some other simple yet thought-provoking game.

Spur of the Moment Family Game Ideas:

- 20 Questions
- What Else?
- I Spy
- I'm Thinking Of

Too Much Togetherness vs. Too Little

The mere sense of living is joy enough.

Emily Dickinson

Too much of anything is often not a good thing. Just as we can spend too little time with our kids, we can also spend too much time. This sounds like a trick statement, I know. But kids need to spend time with friends of their own age, the same as we parents need some time away from kids, having a chance for some interactions aside from those with our children.

Occasionally parents come in on the far end of the parenting spectrum, being either too self-absorbed with work and personal time or too overprotective of their children. Neither is good. While we want to spend ample, quality time with our children, we all, parent and child, need some alone time in addition to peer time. In any relationship, as well as a parent-child relationship, time is needed for short breaks with time to recharge oneself.

There are kids who seem especially needy and who don't want to play alone. It will benefit both child and parent if they are encouraged, little by little, to entertain themselves. Find some solitary activities to engage your child, such as reading, using art and craft materials or finding fun by exploring the backyard. You will probably have to engage in these activities initially, but your child should learn to enjoy these activities on his own. It will certainly help your child in the long run, as this starts to build independence even at an early age.

I recall one mom, in particular, who has hovered constantly over her child, from the time of birth. This child is now eleven, and there is rarely an activity, to this day, that does not involve mother and child or father and child. There are not many independent activities this child engages in with peers. Encourage kids to play with friends their own age as this develops social interaction and actually prepares them to deal with other people and interact appropriately as they grow into adults.

Our Advice:

- Spend time with your children, but balance with some alone time for you and also for your child.

- Give your child your attention; however, do encourage independent play.

- Make sure your children get time to play with other children their age.

- Help your child to find a hobby that is something she really enjoys. This can sometimes carry through to an adult hobby as well.

Dream Big

If you can dream it, you can do it.

Walt Disney

As children we have grand ideas and big dreams. We believe anything is possible. We skip instead of walk. We sing or dance because we feel like it. We are generally happy.

Yet as we get older, more and more people discourage us from dreaming big dreams, and instead tell us to dream about safe things or a sure bet. We are told to be quiet and stop fidgeting. Why are you smiling, smirking or laughing? This is a serious topic.

We are told about responsibilities and what we have to do and what we "should be." How sad is it that parents, caregivers, and teachers often break, or weaken, a child's spirit, or crush his dreams without even knowing it?

It is our job to guide our children, to be positive role models, to provide for them, but it is also our job to try and guide their spirit and help them learn to work hard and gain skills so they can achieve their full potential. What if someone had told the

Wright Brothers or Martin Luther King, Jr. to forget about big dreams?

We have to encourage our children to believe that one day greater and bigger things are possible. Of course, we must also teach our children the importance of a strong work ethic and the importance of education.

The new movie Avatar was a dream that took over twelve years to come true. The script for Avatar was considered over twelve years ago, but they were not able to create the movie then because special effects and technology were not advanced enough. But over the past three years a production team was able to create the first ever virtual camera and using traditional filming of human movement and CGI (Computer Animation) it was finally possible to create Avatar. What if that team did not dream of making that project possible?

George Lucas dreamed of worlds and creatures that did not exist, but he had a vision and made his worlds come alive for millions of people, as did Walt Disney. You see, dreamers when given the encouragement and skills can make anything happen when they work hard and focus their abilities.

Your job as a parent, or grandparent, or adult in the lives of children, is to encourage and foster that child's abilities, creativity, and dreams. Look for ways to say yes or to build your child's confidence and curiosity. Every child has the potential inside of them to make amazing things happen. It is our job to show them the way.

Ways You Can Encourage Your Child to Dream:

- Praise your child's talents.

- Instill a "you can do anything" attitude in your child, not in an arrogant way but in a self-confident way.

- Encourage your child to try new things.

- Teach the importance of a good work ethic, stressing the fact that Dreams and Rewards come from hard work.

- Take advantage of the internet and find new hobbies and activities for your child to experience. Creative activities and printables are available on sites such as Parenting.com, ZiggityZoom.com and FamilyFun.com

Sleepless Nights in Parentville

The one thing children wear out faster than shoes is parents.

John J. Plomp

The truth is you never know what the next hour, much less the next 24, 48 or 72 hours, will hold for you or your kids. You should sleep when you can and try to get a reasonable amount of sleep as often as possible. When your child is a baby, that might be difficult, and your sleep may be choppy. But as your kids get older, sleep will usually improve. The challenge is an unexpected sickness that will keep you and a child up one night or a business project or school commitment that will keep you up late on another occasion. You have to be rested so that when the unexpected keeps you up for a night or multiple nights, you have the endurance and patience to handle the situation and be there for your child.

It is easy to drain your emotional and mental reserves. Find a way to reenergize yourself through rest. Take a break from family and work to pray, meditate, exercise, or visit with a friend. Find help if that is what you need so you can function without being at the end of your fuse with your kids or spouse.

Build Up Your Stamina:

- Get to bed as early as possible. Sleep is your ally.

- Eat a healthy diet. Delete sugar as much as possible, as this promotes fatigue, crankiness and inflammation.

Eat Your Wheaties

Once you choose hope, anything's possible.
Christopher Reeve

Along with getting enough sleep, you need to nourish yourself and your kids with healthy foods to keep your energy level up all day long. Skipping lunch, or a meal, will only add to shorter nerves and exhaustion. With kids you need every extra ounce of energy you can muster. Take it from us: Eat your Wheaties, your veggies, and limit any junk food in your diet.

Imagine a top athlete trying to perform without being properly nourished. He would experience injuries, exhaustion, and poor performance. You need to be nourished to care for yourself and others. And make sure your kids are getting proper nutrition. If affording healthy food for your family is a problem, please ask for help. There are programs in every city and school system that can help families with healthy meals.

Recommendations:

- Don't skip meals.

- Stock your cupboards with healthy snacks.

- Supplement your diet with multiple vitamins, if needed, since there are many times that we are lacking in essential vitamins and minerals.

- Make sure both you and your kids get plenty of fresh air, exercise, and sunshine on a regular basis.

Light at the End of the Tunnel

A little more persistence, a little more effort, and what seemed hopeless failure may turn to glorious success.

Elbert Hubbard

Remember that sleepless nights or exhausting days (due to sickness, a deadline, teenagers, etc...) will not last forever.

As the bible says, "there is a time for every season" and all things will pass, and our stresses or difficulties of today will be distant memories as time passes. Try to remember that embracing the positive and looking at the bigger picture will help to get you through the rough patches. You will have challenges and struggles raising children, but that is true with everything in life. Find the common ground and remember what is truly important. Get up and keep moving forward.

Helpful Reminders:

- Keep a positive outlook.

- Put everything in perspective.

- Try to find something good in everything that happens, regardless of how bad it may seem at the time. This is a learned behavior, and the more we practice it, the more we can look at things this way.

Who's in Control of the Canoe?

The thing that impresses me most about America is the way parents obey their children.

Edward, Duke of Windsor 1957

It's amazing to me how many young families I encounter where it is apparent that the child is in charge. When my cousin had her first child, she and her husband gave in to their toddler all the time. The child even dictated when they went somewhere, where they went, and how long they stayed. What's wrong with this picture?

All kids need guidance and kind discipline, and they need to know you are in charge. Believe it or not, it makes a child more secure if they know what to expect. Parents need to establish routines and guidelines. This will help your child maneuver through his daily life if he knows what is expected of him. Liken your child to a boat that is tethered. If a storm comes along and the boat isn't securely tethered, it will go adrift. Who knows where it will end up? Your child, likewise, needs to have his bearings because if he is allowed too much freedom and does what he wants all the time, he will actually be floundering. This may well show up as bad behavior, talking back, and general disrespect.

Who's in Control Checklist:

- Are you making the rules?

- Is there a routine in your household most days?

- Do you expect respect and give respect?

- Have you established appropriate consequences for disobedience, misbehavior, disrespect, and rules being broken? Parents need to consider possible scenarios for children ahead of time so that when a situation arises, you are able to calmly deal with your child and her poor behavior and give the appropriate consequence.

Going Off Course

The child supplies the power but the parents have to do the steering.

Dr. Benjamin Spock

Parenting is a shared responsibility when there are two parents involved in the raising of children. One parent can't just act like a friend and expect the other parent to "act" like the parent. This may sound odd, but there are some parents who try to be friends so their kids will like them.

In a two-parent family, both parents should try to be in agreement on major points relating to raising the children. Mom and dad, in other words, need to be in the same canoe! But whether it is a two-parent family or a one-parent family, parents need to stay on course by establishing house rules and following expected patterns of discipline that they have laid down. Children learn through daily routine and knowing what the rules are. It is much easier to act as expected once you know the rules. Parents need to instill the rules and follow through.

Nothing is more divisive than if one parent says one thing and the other parent says the opposite. Kids pick up on this very early on and play one parent against the other. A united parenting effort is essential for cohesive parenting that works.

Our Advice:

- Discuss your parenting strategies as a couple.

- Stay in agreement on major issues.

- Don't buckle under persistent begging.

- Communicate directly with your spouse, not through your children. Take the conversation elsewhere or discuss differences at another time.

Over the WaterFall

Risk more than others think is safe.
Care more than others think is wise.
Dream more than others think is practical.
Expect more than others think is possible.

Cadet Maxim

It is time to peel back our many layers of fear or disappointment. Stop living in a safe zone. Life is too darn short for that. It is time to wake up and live. If you taught your child nothing more than to love and respect others, dream big, work hard, give back, and go for it, you will have done your job. Do not let your insecurities, fear, or disappointments taint your child. We are creatures who are continually evolving and growing. Don't get stuck in a rut and stop growing and stretching yourself. Just because you are a parent does not mean you know everything, or that you are supposed to tread water. You are supposed to swim and continue to reach for the shoreline. The target is constantly moving, and you have to keep getting up and going for it.

Our Advice:

- Make goals, however small.

- Encourage your children daily.

- Try new adventures with your family.

Have a Life Preserver

What a child doesn't receive he can seldom later give.

P.D. James, Time to Be in Earnest

Many of us carry the tools of our trade with us when we go to work. For example, a lifeguard goes to work with a whistle, buoy, and radio. A firefighter wears protective gear and brings along water to put out the fire. Yet, often, we do not consider parenting a job, even though it is really a lifelong job where we are on duty, or on call, "twenty-four-seven." As a parent, we need to fill our lives with the tools of the parenting trade. One of those tools is a life preserver, referring to the people, information, or things that can keep our kids healthy and safe from harm.

Specific tools we should fill our tool chest with are "experts" with whom we will need to consult during our child's many years while living at home. One such person is a pediatrician or family doctor. We should find a doctor with whom we are comfortable. We must be able to ask questions and reach the doctor when a concern, emergency, or problem arises. Other experts you may need to consult, or work with, once you have a child are teachers. As you regularly get updates from your child's teacher throughout the year, you will learn of challenges, concerns and strengths your child demonstrates in school. Staying involved will help you be a more aware and supportive parent.

Along with having experts with whom to consult, it is important that parents become informed about child safety, healthy eating, environmental issues, signs of illness, and developmental stages. Of course, parents may not be experts on all of those topics, but by reading credible and current articles, books and listening to talks from experts, you can learn enough to make well-informed decisions for your family.

As parents, we need to be pro-active. There are many things that affect your child's health and well-being, so it is essential for parents to keep abreast of situations and environmental issues that may have a possible effect on your children. Resources, including books and websites, can be a parent's life preserver.

Besides environmental concerns, diet and food allergies are two other sets of issues that parents need to monitor. It is a well-known fact that what your children eat can affect them emotionally, mentally, and physically. Even imperceptible food allergies can make a child moody, irritable, or contribute to learning problems. Certain foods can even affect your child's ability to concentrate. Read up on current studies and stay abreast of food and product recalls.

It is also important that parents be aware of what children watch and view on the television, computer, movie theatre, video games, music, and reading materials. Often children can get a hold of inappropriate materials, age restricted video games, movies or music, or can search or find information that children have no business finding on the internet. It is your job, as the parent, to monitor, and know, what your children do. You are in charge, and you must make this clear and not waiver. Your child's room is not their private abode, so go into it often. This does not mean you are trying to intimidate them, as everyone needs a space to get away from daily pressures. But in order to keep your child safe, you must know what is going on with your child, in your house, and notice when, and if, something seems to change and learn why.

We recommend that all parents keep computers and televisions in common areas of the house and regularly check the computer to see what sites your child has been visiting. Parents need to establish proper guidelines for their kids before they begin using computers to surf the internet, and using social media sites by setting house rules.

Computer and Television Time is a privilege and use should be limited, as well as used only after all homework, chores, and other responsibilities are finished.

You, as the parent, have the right to, and should regularly, review content on your children's computer as long as they are a minor, or as long as they live in your house.

Explain to your child the threats of using social media sites, chat rooms, and email. Explain such things as strangers contacting them or trying to be their online friend, cyber-bullying, posting content (images or language) that are not appropriate or that may cause them to be denied entrance to a college or prevent them from getting hired for a job.

You may need to go online and watch videos or attend a class about how to monitor and check your child's computer. Learn about things such as checking their web browser history, facebook or myspace accounts, images on their hard drive and chat and email conversations.

Included at the end of this book is an excellent list of resources that will help you in your parenting journey. We have also included recommendations for specialists in some specific areas. We can all use as much help as possible in our parenting voyage, and we encourage parents, at all stages, to take advantage of the plethora of resources that are available. Remember, there is no need to "reinvent" the wheel. Even though each and every child will be different, many parenting skills can be learned from other parents who have gone through lots of different experiences.

Be Pro-active:

- Read current articles and books on health updates that might apply to your family.

- Develop a good relationship with your child's pediatrician.

- Communicate with your child's teacher, keeping up to date with your child's progress in school.

- Stay informed on environmental issues, medical updates, product recalls, and food allergy issues.

- Take advantage of the many free resources on the internet and provided at the end of this book.

Wild Things

When my kids become wild and unruly, I use a nice, safe playpen. When they're finished, I climb out.

Erma Bombeck

When your kids get wild and you are running out of patience, you need coping mechanisms and parenting techniques. There are often two things happening at this point. One, the kids haven't had enough physical exercise. Two, you are probably trying to get something accomplished yourself and haven't really guided your child/children into an activity that is engaging. We're not talking about putting them in front of the television either.

Should you have to entertain your kids all the time? Certainly not, but, as the parent, you're in charge and just like being in charge at the office or at work, you need to do some planning, organizing of tasks, and overseeing. Remember ... the kids are not in charge of the kids.

Consider your child's day and determine if she needs to move her body. Or does she need something new and exciting to do? Pull things out of the "Out of the Box" Fun box, try a new art project or craft. Your "out of the box" fun box should contain simple games, special art supplies and other creative activities that are not available on a daily basis. This is why it is such an "up your sleeve" bit of parenting magic. We also like to keep some printouts in the box of ideas for outdoor and indoor games. These can be obtained at websites such as **FamilyFun.com** and **ZiggityZoom.com**.

Note to parents: If your child has a medical condition, such as ADHD, you will know your child's patterns and be given additional ideas to work with your child based on her medical condition.

What to Do:

- Make a List of Things to Do that you can refer to at times.

- Stock creative supplies, books and games.

- Have physical activities that kids can do outside or inside if weather is bad.

- Be prepared to join some of the activities with your kids.

No! No! Stop That

Children seldom misquote. In fact, they usually repeat word for word what you shouldn't have said.

Author Unknown

Your vocabulary will change once you have kids. Many of the words you use will go along with the age of your child. When your kids are very young, you will talk about and use many words related to diapers, going to the bathroom, sleep, eating and development. Once your kids hit their teen years the vocabulary you use will revolve around money, responsibility, peer pressure, friends, permission, and travel. Many of the things you say will be words to express your love and affection for your child.

Sometimes adults find that they may use inappropriate language when upset or frustrated. Guess what? Your child will begin using those suggestive, crude words. So learn to clean up your language now and try your best not to set a bad example for your child. Kids who think it is cool or acceptable to use crude or curse words will find that the opinion of them will be less than desired as they make friends or try and get a job.

In regards to using the word "No" in parenting, remember that just like anything that is overused, it can become something that is ignored. If you find yourself using negatives all the time, try to reassess your language and turn your sentences into positives while still getting your meaning across to your kids.

Finding other Options:

- Maybe.

- Let's Talk about it.

- Perhaps it would be better ...

- If you find yourself using an inappropriate word quite often, make a conscious effort to replace that word with one you would find acceptable for your child to use.

Kids Read Your Body Language

My life is my message.

Ghandi

Body language says a lot. You are often demonstrating the concept "No"even when you don't say it. Be aware of your facial expressions and body language when you interact with others. The more aware you are of your body language and facial expressions the more likely you are to be in control of what you do with your looks and body. Kids and adults read each other's body language and expressions. Even very young children can tell when you appear upset, angry, happy or sad. So make sure your body sends the message you want it to send.

No is an overused word when it comes to kids. Try this experiment. Get 2 jars and a bag of dried beans (or pennies). Label one jar "No" and the other "Yes". Every time you tell your kids NO, Stop that, don't do that, or you put them in time-out or give them a punishment, put a bean in the No jar. And each time you encourage your kids, empower them, redirect without using No, or use positive reinforcement, put a bean in the other jar. Usually the jar with the NO will have a ton of beans in it compared to the jar with the Yes on it. We are often unaware of the number of times we correct and discourage our kids compared to the number of times we encourage and use positive words with them.

If you can become aware of how often you tell your kids NO or 'stop that' or don't do something, you can change the way you approach dealing with your kids and their behavior.

Instead of immediately using negative words like NO, consider the situation and how you could say yes or redirect your child to encourage the right behavior instead of focusing on the wrong behavior.

Our job is to encourage our children. We need to set safe limits and rules for our kids but often parents can be too rigid with behavior or activities that are not deal breakers.

Of course, behavior that can potentially cause harm to your child, or someone else, needs to be stopped immediately and other house rules need to be upheld, but often we could take a different approach to how we handle certain situations.

For instance, if your child is jumping on the furniture you might tell them to STOP or say NO Jumping on the furniture without even thinking about why they are doing it.

Instead, stop yourself, and go through this exercise.

Ask yourself these questions:

1. Why might my kids be doing this?

2. What are my options?

3. How can I encourage, teach or be positive even in this situation?

Encouraging Good Behavior

No act of kindness, no matter how small, is ever wasted.

Aesop

I may see my kids jumping on the furniture and realize that they have been stuck in the house all day and need to get outside to burn off some energy and get moving. So I will quickly think of a game or activity they can do that will use up some energy while playing the game or activity, or I will send them outside without even saying 'No Jumping'. Or I can ask them a question like, "Where Do We Jump?" or "Are we supposed to be jumping on the furniture?" Obviously, we have a "no jumping on the furniture" rule in our house, but when the kids have not had a chance to get any exercise these things do happen on occasion.

If I needed to, I would then tell them the rule and what I want them to DO not tell them what I DO NOT want them to do. I could say, "When we want to Jump we use our feet to jump on the floor or go outside". You can even give them an option ... would you rather bring the jumping down to the floor or go outside and jump on the grass? This is a better option instead of thinking to yourself that they know they aren't allowed to jump on the furniture and they are doing it to spite me or even though they know better. Kids don't usually think like that. It is usually more innocent than that and fulfills an immediate gratification for them without much forethought.

Remember the more you abuse using the word NO ... STOP THAT ... Don't Do That ... the less impact it will have. The boy who cried wolf is a story you should keep in your head. No one wants to be told something negative over and over again. What if your boss did that to you?

Lock up the word NO and replace it with "**Why Not**?" or **Go**. Kids will often get rowdy and break a rule when you are busy doing something else. You need to recognize the behavior as a sign to find an activity that will engage your kids.

You, as the parent, are part of the reason for the behavior. Kids need to have a sense of structure, and they need guidance and prompting. It is your job to help them figure out a new activity to do or refocus them when the earlier activity is no longer keeping their interest. We cannot expect our child to be engaged by the same activity all day. If they get disinterested or bored, they are more likely to get into mischief.

Our Advice:

- Have a ready list of indoor and outdoor activities.

- Go online for a printable list of "Out of the Box" fun ideas and free printables at **ZiggityZoom.com**.

- When kids get antsy, rather than get upset, refer to your list and suggest, or prepare, an activity to change the atmosphere of unwanted behavior. Often, all it takes is changing things out a bit.

- Make yourself available to your children. As we all notice, kids start "acting out" when parents are on the phone or busy otherwise.

- List ways that you might **Encourage your kids** and remember to do it often. Refrain from using the "no" word.

When Your Child is No longer Recognizable

In spite of the six thousand manuals on child raising in the bookstores, child raising is still a dark continent and no one really knows anything. You just need a lot of love and luck ... and, of course, courage.

Bill Cosby, Fatherhood, 1986

In regard to teenagers and kids getting ready to go off to college or leave home, there are a few important things to keep in mind. We mention this now as it is always best to have a plan ahead of time.

The years prior to when a child will be leaving your household and your rules are a prime time for what I call "trial freedom". Too often parents are overly strict all the way up to when a child leaves home, and you know what tends to happen when this occurs? The children who were given no freedoms while under parental control, were never allowed to make any decisions or to be responsible for their mistakes are the very ones who go ballistic at their first taste of freedom. This happens to kids going off to college or getting their own apartment. I've seen it happen many times.

Obviously, this isn't true of all kids, but it is certainly worth noting before your child reaches that age. I would much prefer giving any child a little more freedom in learning to make their own decisions and helping to guide them while under my roof.

You can start giving kids choices when they are still very young, and, as they master one concept, give them more responsibility. For instance, allow them to start managing a small monthly allowance during the early elementary years (5-9), and as they get older, give them more direction and money to make other choices. As you give them more responsibility, they will begin to make better choices or learn to live with their choices.

A good example of this is a preteen who learns to use her allowance, or earned money, for the things she needs or wants to buy. She will then be a better steward of her money as she begins driving. For instance, if she needs a tank of gas every month, she had better budget sufficient money for the gas in order to drive the car. Blowing all her money on one sweater will result in having no money to go out the rest of the month. But if you continually give her more money, it will teach her nothing. Parenting often requires us to think ahead in order to decide what we want to teach kids now.

Giving kids responsibility for some of their time, their money, and making choices starts by us teaching them how to make good decisions and then letting them try it with our guidance. We also have to let them make mistakes so they learn how to spend wiser next time or how to plan the best use of their time.

Our Advice:

- Give children responsibilities around the house, starting when they are young. Of course, young children should be only given small jobs, but they will still feel like important jobs to them.

- Let children make decisions, but also let them be responsible for the decisions they choose.

- Guide your kids kindly in this process as there are many teachable moments that will arise.

Follow the Leader

I know of no other success I could attain that would surpass my achievement of raising my children.

Sharon Pierce McCullough

One of the earliest lessons we need to teach children is to follow the leader. In order to function well in our society, it is necessary to accept the fact that, in most situations, someone is in charge. At home, at school, at work, someone always has to be in charge.

Children learn at a very early age that the parent is the one in charge. At least this is the perception that a parent should be conveying. This can get out of whack quickly if we give in to the whims and whines of our children and if we fail to demonstrate our control in a calm, kind, and assertive manner.

By establishing this concept early on, we will help to make a smoother transition when our children start school and eventually get a job. We have all observed kids and adults who have an issue with authority. It is often because they were never taught this concept at home, or their parents, themselves, passed on their own inability to accept authority.

Remember:

- Be a good example to your children.

- Teach your kids to respect authority.

- Be calm, kind and assertive.

Monkey See, Monkey Do

To bring up a child in the way he should go, travel that way yourself once in a while.

Josh Billings

As a parent, it does not work to have a "Do as I say, not what I do" attitude. Kids of all ages are aware of everything you do and everything you say. How many times have you heard a child say something disrespectful or something even worse, such as a swear word? Guess where that came from? Often, it comes from the parent, but sometimes it comes from children watching a show that isn't age-appropriate or even from one of their friends who heard a comment from an older kid.

If we want our children to grow into responsible, caring adults, we need to lead them all along the way. Our example is their primary example and if we have some bad habits of our own, once the kids start arriving is a good time to do a re-evaluation of ourselves. We may just have to clean up our language, getting rid of a few easily said swear words, stop eating pie for breakfast, or having a beer every night. We have to remember that we are now living in a Monkey See Monkey Do world.

Remember:

- You are your Child's best role model and teacher.

- Ask yourself, would I want my child to behave this way?

Little Mimics

Children are natural mimics who act like their parents despite every effort to teach them good manners.

Author Unknown

Kids like to mimic, and if you haven't gone through that stage with your kids yet, you will. For some reason children find it terribly amusing to mimic everything you say or their sibling says. Siblings, of course, find this very annoying.

Keep in mind that your child is absorbing everything around him, cataloging every little thing that is said and heard. If you don't want something repeated do not say it within earshot of your children. It may come back to bite you.

Consider for a moment, the type of adult you want to raise. Now think about what you have taught your child thus far along his journey to adulthood. If you have never considered this before, look at your actions, language and efforts. Do they enforce the values you want to teach your child. For example, do not expect them to treat others with respect if you teach them disrespect by the way you treat them or others.

As parents, we are also responsible for what we allow our children to watch or see on television, what sites they visit on the computer, and other materials that may influence their behavior or have an adverse affect on them. Too many children are allowed to watch movies and shows that are inappropriate for their age. Even babies and toddlers are affected by scenes and sounds they are exposed to at an early age. Many people think young children are oblivious to television or a movie playing in the background, but it can affect their sleep and their interactions with others. Studies have shown that children who view violence on television exhibit more aggression with their peers.

Our Advice:

- Get rid of any bad or rude language

- Treat your child with respect

- Show kindness, respect, and consideration for others

- Take responsibility for your child's behavior (often some of it results from a parent or another family member)

- Monitor what your children watch, or see, on television, DVDs or movies. Stay aware of sites your child visits on the computer and other such devices.

- Know your child's friends and, as they get older, verify your child's whereabouts.

Instilling Good Habits

Don't worry that children never listen to you; worry that they are always watching you.

Robert Fulghum

Children are the most astute observers. They watch us and pay attention to our actions, words, and body language. They know who they feel comfortable with and who they do not like. If we want our kids to grow up to be well-rounded, independent adults who can hold a job, give back to their community, and have fruitful relationships, we need to teach them to be prepared for their future and the day they will be on their own. Often parents wait until their kids are in their teenage years to begin teaching them valuable lessons that they need to succeed. In reality, it is best to start these lessons at a young age.

Building Good Habits:

- Teach young children about money management.

- Give children choices and allow them to make decisions.

- Give older children a budget for the month and do not give them additional money, help them learn to budget for entertainment, clothing, gas, etc.

- Get your child involved in a sport, or activity that will allow them to experience wins and losses.

- Do not give your child every toy, or item they want. When we give in to their every whim, they do not learn to value the items they have.

Teach Them to Be Prepared

A child educated only at school is an undereducated child.

George Santayana

If you have small children, give them bite-size tasks or responsibility and as they learn to handle the small things, give them a little bit more responsibility or a harder task.

We encourage you to teach your children to be prepared for financial independence (how to handle money), doing their own laundry or helping with chores, how to make a meal, volunteering at home. You can also help teach them how to be prepared for school by working on projects, homework and studying for tests.

As parents we need to give our children opportunities to steer the boat and let them take the lead sometimes. Often parents do not let their kids take the lead, or they don't even think about this possibility.

It is also important to get your kids involved in a team sport, extracurricular activity, a club, or scouts. Getting your kids involved and keeping them involved in activities will keep them focused on a positive interest and let them interact with kids that have similar interests. Being involved in a sport or club will give them an opportunity to learn from another adult coach, or facilitator who will encourage them and work with them to practice or work hard to reach a goal, whether it be doing well in a sports game, a tournament, or challenge.

Learning how to be prepared is so important because what we learn as we grow up helps us be able to meet deadlines, prepare for our jobs as adults, and keep ourselves organized.

For kids to reach their full potential, they have to know how the world works and how we go about getting what we want.

If we want to raise children to consider the state of the world and how each of us make decisions every day that impact our lives and the Earth, we need to make smart decisions and talk to our kids about the decisions. It is easy to take small steps that will have a big payoff, both for our communities and in imparting knowledge to our children.

Here are a few examples:

- Do you have a grocery store or shopping center within walking distance to your house? Take a family walk to the store to buy an item or two you need. You can teach the kids how you can save on gas, pollution, and also get some needed exercise.

- Make a meal at home with fresh ingredients or visit a local farm or restaurant that uses fresh local ingredients. Let your kids see the sources of the food they eat. Even better is to start a garden, and let your kids help raise the vegetables they eat.

If we have hopes that our children will help those in our own community, we need to expose them to helping others. Find out which local charities or churches allow kids to volunteer with you or if they are old enough to do volunteer work by themselves.

Decision Making

Try not to be a man of success, but rather try to be a man of value.

Albert Einstein

As hard as it is sometimes, we have to let our children make some of their own decisions. Although mistakes will be made and we can see the wrong decision being made, this is how we all learn.

The process of making decisions and mistakes brings with it the question of accountability and owning up to one's own actions. Children whose parents make every decision and every plan for them continually will thwart their child's decision-making process. I know some young adults in their twenties who are almost incapable of making their own decisions and getting their life organized. Their parents, unfortunately, never encouraged them to make their own decisions

Sometimes we are so busy getting our kids from place to place, we forget to consider what we are teaching them. If we put value on material possessions more so than loving others or helping those that need help, what are we teaching our children? Whether it be a neighbor, or someone less fortunate. Who needs a helping hand, if we don't reach out, then why would we expect our kids to grow up valuing people, compassion, kindness, and hard work? We must teach our kids what is important and not allow the "Keeping up with the Joneses" to become the idea our kids learn from us. It is fine to have nice things, but if money or things become the focus, we are not teaching kids values based on our own beliefs and those that our society needs.

Often parents try to give their children everything they want. In order to teach your child to be a giving, compassionate, and productive adult, you must give them responsibility, allow them to make some mistakes, learn patience, have losses or deal with obstacles, and understand that we have to work hard to get things (a job, a car, home, etc.)

Our Advice:

- Talk openly to your children about values you think are important,

  such as honesty and compassion.

- Let kids make decisions and hold them accountable even with small decisions. Obviously, take into consideration the age of the child.

- Encourage your kids to help in planning family activities. Make it a weekly event.

Your Inner Child

You are worried about seeing him spend his early years in doing nothing. What! Is it nothing to be happy? Nothing to skip, play, run around all day long? Never in his life will he be so busy again.

Jean Jacques Rousseau, Emile, 1762

By keeping in touch with your inner child and a sense of wonder you will make parenting more fun and enjoyable and will raise a happy child.

Children are perfect in their being. They experience true feelings and will express those feelings, whether good, bad or sad feelings. They rush to experience a new or curious activity

My advice to every parent is to play with your kids instead of just watching them play. You will be amazed at how much fun it is and how much more fun you have with your kids. You will truly enjoy them more when you realize parenting is about spending time with your kids, not just rearing children.

By getting into the activity and playing with your kids you are also showing your kids you care, that they are important, and you do have fun with them.

I know from experience how hard it can be to always jump in and just let go of your to-do list, schedule, and concerns, and just live in the moment with your family. Your kids will remember the times you played with them for years to come. They will not remember that you drove them to the pool fifty times, but they will remember the things you did with them. Be hands-on and strip away your adulthood by cutting loose and having some real fun.

Here are ways you can connect with your kids and make memories you and your children will cherish.

1. **Get Involved in Activities with your Kids**
   In the summer, play games in the water with your kids. Play Sharks & Minnows, Marco Polo, and any other water game or even a swim race across the pool. It is simple, but lots of us moms sit on the side line. Hey, even take a lap through the sprinkler when your kids are cooling off. Believe me, the giggles you will hear will be worth the soggy flip flops.

2. **Get Out into Nature or to a Museum**
   Take a hike through a state park, go to a local museum, or go dig in the sand with your kids. Look up at the sky, take in the wonder of nature or man-made art, and talk to your kids. Look for cool birds, or insects, or talk

about the art. Or just dig in the dirt with them. Let your kids guide you.

3. **Play Games** Do not underestimate the value of playing a board game or simple game like I Spy with your child. Besides teaching your child the rules of play, learning to take turns, and patience, you will demonstrate to your child that he is important because you are spending quality time with him. Another option is to read a book with your child. Even if they are an advanced reader, kids enjoy being read to, especially if you can read it with passion or be very animated in your telling.

4. **Try Something New** Take your kids to do something fun that you have never done, or to a place you have never been. Don't let your inexperience keep you from introducing something new to your kids. Go camping, fishing, crabbing, or canoeing. Go ahead, you can do it!

5. **Sing songs** Sing classic or new songs in the car with your kids on a road trip or around a campfire.

6. **Let your Kids Participate** Do you enjoy cooking or taking pictures or painting? Do you ever let your kids give it a try? If not, now is the time to do so. I let my kids help

make muffins, pancakes, dinner meals and other dishes.

7. **Get Crafty or Artsy** Whether you have a creative or crafty bone in your body or not, pull out the construction paper, glue, markers, tape and string and let your kids make something. But be the example of someone who gets in there and makes something. Have fun and be creative, you do have it in you.

8. **Take the Fun Plunge** You can find tons of free printables and ideas for games or even recycling craft projects online. A great resource for fun plunge ideas is on **ZiggityZoom.com**.

At the end of the day, it is about getting down on your child's level, putting your hands in the sand or dirt, and letting go. Let go of the parenting worries and housekeeping qualms for a little while and experience the joy of life. The other day my middle son said, "mom you never get in the pool at Grandma's house, its been like a year." I realized I was not connecting with my kids at the pool. I always had a reason. My mascara might smear or I wanted to relax beside the pool while my kids swam. I realized I was sending the wrong message, and I jumped right in with both feet.

Remember:

- It's okay to take a little parent time, but you have to have some fun time with your kids too. So put down that dish towel and take the Fun Plunge. The memories you and your child make will truly last a lifetime!

Think Like a Child

The great man is he who does not lose his childlike heart."

Mencius

Kids like to have fun. Period. And one way to get our kids to reach their full potential is through encouraging them to be creative.

Have your child try new things. Make sure your child has downtime or time to do what he enjoys. When we have down time we are often our most creative. Our minds are able to be open to ideas. By downtime we do not mean time sitting in front of the TV or playing video games, but time outside, reading, drawing, playing music, doing artwork, problem solving, or relaxing.

When do you think Mozart had time to write Symphonies & Operas?

We need to introduce children to new activities and ideas. Introduce them to art, music, sports, books, food, nature, and science.

Ask yourself this question...

- If I had it to do all over again, what creative pursuit, sport or activity would I have explored? In doing so, perhaps you can introduce your child to this endeavor or another that you both have interest in pursuing.

The Secret to Silliness

There is no duty we so much underrate as the duty of being happy.

                                    Robert Louis Stevenson

Any time you add a bit of silliness or fun to a chore, activity or day, the smoother the task seems to go. If you want your kids to clean their room or do a chore, instead of harping on them and telling them to clean their room multiple times, a technique that often does not work, try a different strategy. Go into their room and show them how to have a bit of fun with it. Grab a container and a few of the toys or clothes to be picked up and start shooting baskets. Tell them how many baskets you made and ask them how many they think they can make.

You need to show them how to have more fun doing the things that have to get done anyway. If you have older kids a simple game may not work. You can try getting them to clean up and then taking a break to shoot baskets for ten minutes outside.

In other words, you need to motivate them. Adding a little bit of fun is going to have big returns for you and your kids.

Teach them how to have fun in their daily lives. Everyone has to do chores but if we make it more fun, life will be more enjoyable.

Try this:

- Get silly with your kids.

- Make some of the housework chores into a game.

Do What You Love

Love life and life will love you back. Love people and they will love you back.

Arthur Rubinstein

One of the things you can instill in your children that will have a profound effect on their entire life is to teach them to seek what it is they truly love to do in life. The people that are the happiest are people who are working at a job or business that they really enjoy. Amazingly, this doesn't have to be a professional job, such as a doctor or a lawyer, because you often hear of people in professional jobs leaving their professions in search of what they love, what they feel they can contribute to society.

If you, yourself, can identify what you love to do, then it may be even easier for your child to follow their hearts. I know this is sometimes a tough concept to accept, especially for someone who has had generations of family members in a long line of the same business or profession. But what we need to remember here is that we are all different, and we all have a different contribution to make. Try to help and encourage your child to find their own way.

But even beyond loving what we do, remember the universal principle to love others. Truly, if more of us went through life showing kindness, compassion and love to each other, it would be a truly better place.

Finding What They Love:

- Constantly offer support and encouragement to your children when they show an interest in something.

- Make your children aware that all people are given different gifts and help them find theirs.

Take a Hike

Must we always teach our children with books? Let them look at the stars and the mountains above. Let them look at the waters and the trees and flowers on Earth. Then they will begin to think, and to think is the beginning of a real education.

David Polis

Life was not meant to be lived only on paved streets and inside of walls. We must get outside and live our days in green space with trees and open fields. Our bodies were meant to move and, with today's obligations of work, school, and the way many of our existing communities are designed, many of us can go days, weeks or even years without venturing outside to enjoy the beauty of this world.

Our perspectives change when we remove ourselves from our daily routines of office spaces and inside our homes to experience all the wonder and beauty of nature. Our mood and perspective quickly changes once we can enjoy the nature around us. Take time to get outside, sit on a bench or lay on the grass and just enjoy the day. Watch the reeds move with the wind or the birds and animals pass by. Take a walk with your kids or have a picnic outside.

We quickly realize life is about much more than ourselves. Just as it is important to make time to spend with your family, it is important to get outside. Introduce your children to the amazing greatness of nature.

Make your kids and family a top priority. Kids will suffer if parents are adult-only oriented and time-schedule sensitive. We, as parents, need to respond to needs of children. Yes, children do have needs that should be met, just as we, as adults, also do. We are speaking needs, not wants and whims here.

Our Advice:

- Plan weekly outings with your family. Try to include as many varied outside activities as feasible.

- Make sunshine, exercise, and fresh air a priority for both mental and physical well being.

Leave Your Work at the Door

Your children need your presence more than your presents.

Jesse Jackson

Work is a necessary part of life. Each of us will have work to do, whether we work for a company, ourselves or work in the home. The question is not whether or not we work, but how we balance our lives.

All of us spend countless hours working every week. If you work outside of the home you are likely gone for forty to eighty hours a week working, or traveling to work. For those of you who work in the home, the responsibilities of running a household take up much of your time.

You must learn to set work-life boundaries , making sure to schedule quality time with your family. If you work in the home, you may want to set a schedule so that house work, meals, planning, organizing and making payments do not overwhelm every waking second.

In either of the above circumstances, you need to learn to turn off the computer, the cell phone, the television, and mark off time to spend with your family. Spend dinner together talking, play a game, take a walk, or go play ball.

Sometimes we get so wrapped up in the day and our responsibilities that we do not consider the message we are sending to our children. We are actually ignoring them when we send them away to watch tv, or to do something on their own so we can clean, catch up on work, or spend time watching a favorite tv program. We need to commit to spending time with our kids. We need to make time when come first. Ignore or turn off, the phone, the tv, and computer. Ask your child what she would like to do.

It is also important to set up special times to spend with each of your kids alone, and, if you have a spouse, to set up regular date nights for couple time.

An important way to connect with each family member and make them feel special is to schedule monthly dates with your child so you can fit in one-on-one time. You might consider picking what the two of you do one month and then allowing your child or spouse to pick the next month. Of course, you may have to give your child a few options from which to choose that are reasonable and affordable. Consider if it is a school night or weekend type of activity.

Family Time Suggestions:

- Schedule time into each day for "family time" even if it will only be fifteen minutes some days.

- Have days of the week for mandatory "family dinners." This is so important to building family unity.

A Balancing Act - Be Consistent

Happiness is not a matter of intensity but of balance and order and rhythm and harmony.

Thomas Merton

You have to determine the appropriate actions to take when your child breaks the rules. Will you first give a warning for misbehavior, and the next time a consequence? It is best to know what the process will be so that when a situation arises you can go through the same steps every time. Otherwise, your frustration can lead you to shouting, and acting out of anger, and giving a consequence that is not in line with the behavior. Be consistent and follow through with an appropriate consequence when your child breaks the rules. It might be a warning and then redirect if they are in preschool. For an elementary school-aged child, you may use take away a privilege or give a timeout.

There will be times when kids do not follow the rules. Often redirecting a child to something else, or giving them an appropriate time out or consequence for the rule breaking or misbehavior will resolve the behavior. But more often than not, if our children continue to misbehave there is a reason.

Often, because parents do not clearly set the rules of the house, and determine appropriate consequences for not following the rules, when children misbehave, parents can become frustrated or angry and overreact. As a parent, you can get so upset that you may actually be the one that needs a time out. You may need to remove yourself from the situation to cool off. If you find your blood pressure rising and yourself getting angry or overly frustrated, go out of the room and take a few deep breaths. Unless your children are in a dangerous situation, you can take a moment to calm down, get composed, and think about what just happened. Once you have yourself together, you can go back in with your child and handle the behavior. Your actions will be more appropriate and your child will stay calmer because you are calm. You are now teaching your child that it is more important to regroup, to think through what we do and say than to overreact, scream or get so angry. There is a healthy way to handle children and the stress that poor behavior can cause. Remember that it is our job to keep ourselves calm and to focus and think before we act. We should keep the behavior in perspective because often it is not as bad as we feel it is at the moment.

Our advice:

- Set House Rules.

- Determine age-appropriate discipline.

- Be consistent with your actions and follow through.

- Remove yourself from the situation if you are angry or overly frustrated.

- Do not give idle threats as this undermines your parental authority.

Be a Story Teller

"Do You Remember When..." bonds people together more than shared chromosomes. Stories are thicker than blood.

Daniel Taylor

I am sure you have that one uncle or friend that has the gift of storytelling. Those people that can command the attention of everyone in the room and somehow make them laugh and cry within a matter of minutes. They have a gift for storytelling. Although we are not all born storytellers, sharing stories and making our own family stories is something that every generation has done. As a parent it is important for us to understand the effect that sharing a story or family experience has on us and our children. Can you remember any family stories from when you were growing up or from years past when you gathered with your loved ones? Usually it is the stories that make us laugh, cry, or embarrassed that we remember and often retell year after year. Well, stories start with taking the time to sit with our family to tell a story. It can be reading a story or verbally acting out a favorite story, a made-up story or a story about our youth, or something our child did when he or she was very young. The idea is to encourage sharing time together and to begin to make our own family stories from the times spent together. Any gathering can be a time to tell stories or make family memories that will become worthy of a family story.

A great example for my family occurred on the last camping trip we took. We were with nine other families camping and it was the middle of the day on a Saturday. The skies were sunny and the day warm. We noticed the winds picking up and off in the distance there was a darkness creeping towards us. We checked the weather report and sure enough, a storm was heading towards us quickly. Before we were aware that a storm was coming, my husband and youngest son had gone in the car to the store. I was there with my five and seven-year-old boys and our friends. The winds whipped up and the rain began to fall so we headed for our tent. As soon as I got the zipper closed on the tent, the wind became so strong it was pushing the front of the tent over onto us. It was, literally, crushing the tent into us. I was yelling to my brother who was in the tent next to us, and he was trying to get out of his tent too. I had a hard time getting the zipper open, but, when I did, we made a run for a friend's pop-up camper. We scrambled inside with a friend and her kids. Her husband and my brother went to help our friends secure their tent that had collapsed. I began videotaping the story. All of our kids were crying and screaming. They were very scared. All of a sudden I saw a tent flying by us due to the strong winds. It was heading towards the small lake nearby. All of the guys we were with ran after it and finally stopped it. Just as quickly as the heavy rain and squall winds came, they were gone. Left was a swampland of broken, dripping wet tents. Fortunately, other than the tent that flew away and some broken poles, everyone was okay, just a bit shaken up and waterlogged. But wow, we had some serious material for a one-of-a-kind family story. First, my husband was gone and safely away from the campsite in a car for starters. Then my five-year-old saying he never wanted to go camping again plus some other classic lines. Don't forget that the tent went flying through the air and the rescues. There was so much to tell. Fortunately, my boys have been camping since then without any further trauma from that day. As they get older, that story will be told and retold, and we will laugh about that experience and how crazy it was. That is one of their first camping experiences, and- wow- what a story it was! The winds were reaching sixty MPH gusting at us off the water.

Encourage Family Storytelling:

- Read to your children starting when they are babies.

- Encourage your kids to "tell about" things they experience.

- Take turns at the dinner table creating a "story" with each person adding something to the story.

Seize the Day

You will never find time for anything. If you want time you must make it.

Charles Buxton

We do not know what tomorrow will hold for us or our loved ones. That statement is not said to make us fearful, but for us to consider that today we should tell the ones we love how much we care, and experience the things in life we believe are worthwhile.

It is time to get in touch with yourself, your emotions, and your dreams. Stop burying them deep within. Now is the time to tell your children, whether young or grown, that you love them, and how proud you are of them. Now is the time to take that trip to Italy or France, or wherever you have wanted to visit. Look for what makes you happy and go in that direction. With some planning and kindness, you could live your days in happiness instead of settling. And by doing so you are teaching your children an important lesson in life.

Besides loving others, live with passion, and do what you were meant to do.

Ways to Seize the Day:

- Tell your children you love them each and every day.

- Enjoy your family NOW ... don't procrastinate.

- Live in the present.

Be a Life Long Learner

A child can ask questions that a wise man cannot answer.

Author Unknown

We have all heard the saying that a parent is a child's first teacher. Often it is easy for a parent to forget a child is always learning from his parents. Can you remember those teachers who had the biggest impact on you? Whether it was a parent, teacher, or coach, that person was probably able to instill in you their own enthusiasm or passion for a subject or activity. He/she most likely believed strongly in you, and believed you were capable of even more than you yourself knew you were.

Throughout life it will be necessary to learn new things for work, in your personal life, and to grow with the world. Look at how much technology has changed in the last twenty-five years. There is data showing that, as we age, those of us who challenge our minds with new activities and experiences live longer and have less occurrences of Alzheimer's.

Lifelong learners are happier people.

Suggestion:

- Make a list of things you would like to learn or do. Work on making it happen.

- Find exciting new challenges and activities for you and your children to do together. Find out activities some of your friends families are enjoying if you are stumped.

What Happened to Privacy?

Answering questions is a major part of sex education. Two rules cover the ground. First, always give a truthful answer to a question; secondly, regard sex knowledge as exactly like any other knowledge.

Bertrand Russell

The fact of the matter is that from the time you are expecting your first child until your kids are grown, your modesty will go out the window. For moms-to-be, we find out at our prenatal visits that we had better just relax when it comes to being half-dressed in front of our doctors. When it's time to deliver our baby, we might feel a bit modest or embarrassed about having our legs grabbed and having to push out our baby. Those thoughts quickly evaporate when your body alerts you to the fact that your baby wants out. Once the baby is on his way, fluids, cord and all, embarrassment quickly fades. You will have turned your focus to the miracle you have just delivered. When you have to go in to use the bathroom and a nurse accompanies you, you will soon realize that this is a typical day for them. There is little room for modesty once you are admitted to the maternity ward.

Once you bring your baby home, all remaining modesty flies out the door. If you choose to breast feed your baby, this presents another set of potentially awkward situations. We highly recommend breast feeding, as both of us breast fed all of our babies. Of course, we all have various challenges with which to contend when there are visitors stopping by and when you are out in public with the baby. Just remember, baby comes first. Breastfeeding is a natural way to feed your child, so do not let anyone make you or your spouse feel uncomfortable. Get help from a lactation specialist and read some of the many available books on the subject.

We respect the fact that each woman has to decide how to nourish her own baby. No one should be made to feel that they have to breastfeed, especially if they are uncomfortable doing so. The important thing to remember is to make your baby feel loved and secure.

Our Advice:

- Try to retain your modesty, but go with the flow when things happen that might normally make you uncomfortable, such as a child popping into the shower unexpectedly or into your bedroom.

- Remember that kids won't think much about seeing a parent unclothed if the parent doesn't make a big deal out of it. And, of course, some parents encourage nudity from

the start.   Do whatever makes you most
comfortable.

The Birds & the Bees

Human beings are the only creatures on earth that
allow their children to come back home.

Bill Cosby

Let's talk about Sex.   Each parent has different
levels of comfort when it comes to talking about
human sexuality.   For many of us, our religious
beliefs likely play into our feelings of human
sexuality.   Regardless of how you personally feel
about when intimacy is appropriate, (ex. after
marriage only), a parent needs to discuss the
anatomy of the human body with their children.
You need to be able to answer questions about
situations that may arise and to address peer
pressure your children may encounter regarding
intimacy.   Even if you closely monitor your child
every to ensure there is little chance of kissing,
touching or more, he/she still needs to be informed.
In order to raise a confident, knowledgeable adult,
children need to know how the body works, and
what is appropriate, or inappropriate, based on
your values.

In other words, you need to be comfortable and understanding when discussing human anatomy and sexuality. Each family will tell their children what is appropriate for their beliefs and value systems. The important part is having open communication so your kids will come to you to ask about their changing bodies and the changes they notice in kids around them.

Our Advice:

- Answer questions, as they arise, to the best of your ability.

- Consider the age of the child asking the question and tailor your answers to their level of understanding.

- Research available books on this subject and use them when the time seems appropriate. Some questions start at a very early age, depending on the child and their playmates.

At the End of the Day

We worry about what a child will become tomorrow, yet we forget that he is someone today.

Stacia Tauscher

At the end of the day, what really matters is that we have loved our children, used our resources, acted kindly, and guided the best we could. We all make mistakes, and wish we'd done some things differently, but what is truly important boils down to two things ... Love and Kindness. As long as we try to continue along that path, our children will know that we love and care for them. We have done our best.

What is important is loving our children, teaching them how to be kind, loving and how to adapt. Life will throw us curve balls and those of us that are prepared to handle the curve ball and look for a different path or answer will do well.

Spend time with the ones you love and live life. Work and money should not be what defines us, we must remember living is about relationships, love and experiences, not how hard you worked or how much money you have accumulated. When you are gone, your position will be replaced, your money will be worth nothing to you, but the love and memory of you that others have will live on.

Remember:

- Be thankful.
- Be kind.
- Be forgiving.

Home Sweet Home

The ache for home lives in all of us, the safe place where we can go as we are and not be questioned.

Maya Angelou

Whether young or old, we all want a place to belong. The world can sometimes be hard and cruel, but all of us should be able to find a safe haven in our home. Occasionally children make big mistakes, but mistakes do not define them. Your daughter may embarrass you, or you may disapprove of how she lives her life, but she will always be your daughter. Show her you love her and that she is accepted. We all want to be loved and accepted. One of the hardest jobs you may have is accepting your adult child if you cannot accept her for who she is and who she becomes. Love will conquer all if you open your heart and let it in.

Of course, we do not mean that you should let your child live with you forever, but have an open heart, listening ear, and willingness to be there for them. Remember, your child's home will forever be wherever you are. Yes, they will make their own home eventually, but there is a part of them that will always reside with you, the parent.

Be Present

Do not dwell in the past, do not dream of the future, concentrate the mind on the present moment.

Buddha

Be present in the current moment. It is easy to keep ourselves occupied thinking about what happened yesterday or worrying about everything we need to get done for tomorrow. When we allow ourselves to be preoccupied by the past or the future, we often miss what is happening right now. We need to reel in our thoughts, concerns and worries to focus on what is going on around us right now. When we get involved in the present, we will experience more joy and amazing opportunities to connect with our kids, our spouse, or friends.

Life will happen around you and in order to fully appreciate it, you must be real, present, and open. Your child needs you present in his life. You have lessons to teach him, love to give, and guidance to offer. If you have a tendency to retreat or look inwards when life gets tough, it will be harder for you to be open and honest with your child as challenges arise.

Remember that children grow up too quickly, and we have to take every lovely moment God gives us and make the most of them.

Unconditional Love

"Children need love, especially when they do not deserve it."

Harold Hulbert

Strive to love your child unconditionally. I believe that, even if showing love doesn't come naturally to a parent it can become a learned behavior. We can practice showing unconditional love even when our children aren't particularly good on a given day or our day is filled with stress. Let your child know, regardless, that you love them ... that you will always love them ... until the end of time.

You Can Never Say, "I Love You," Too Much

There is only one happiness in life, to love and be loved.

George Sand

As a parent we have an opportunity to be an example to our child of what a healthy, loving relationship looks like. Tell your child you love them as often as you like. If you are someone who struggles with expressing your feelings, then make it a goal for yourself to tell those you love that you love them or show them with a hug, kiss, or pat on the back. You might even put reminders around the house to prompt you to show signs of affection. We can also tell our children or spouse we love them by putting love notes in their lunch boxes or on their pillows, or by going on a special date with them. There has been plenty of research done in this area that supports showing love and affection to children and the positive effects it has on them. Children in orphanages that are rarely held or loved often have difficulties and can experience delayed growth. Affection and human touch is a human necessity, but it is one most of us in the United States seldom think about.

It is also important that our kids see adults in positive, healthy, loving relationships with other adults. If you are married, showing affection for your spouse is important. If not married, your kids need to see you interact with other adults affectionately or observe other family or friends in loving relationships.

Thankfulness

Appreciation is the highest form of prayer, for it acknowledges the presence of good wherever you shine the light of your thankful thoughts.

Alan Cohen

Today, more than ever before, it can be difficult to remember to be thankful for what we have and to teach thankfulness to our children. With the availability and ease of every imaginable product we could ever want, it can be hard to remember to give thanks for the love, family, friendship and things we have in life. If you are a religious person, then you may make a more concerted effort to give thanks to God for all you have and have been given which is a wonderful thing. If you are not, then you may need to start thinking about how blessed you are. Either way, it is important to teach our children to be thankful for what they have, instead of always wanting more. We should all be thankful for our family, friendships, and what blessings we have been given, no matter how much or how little we have materially. It is easy to put too much focus on material possessions as they truly have no lasting value. They are convenient, but they will not satisfy our heart and soul.

We can teach our children to be thankful by letting everyone take turns at dinner, or bedtime, sharing the things for which they are thankful. You do not need to correct them. Any answer is acceptable. It is an exercise to get the whole family thinking about why they are thankful. The more you and your children do this, the easier it will be for them to think of meaningful answers for themselves.

It is also important to talk about what they have that many others do not have and how your family can help others. The point of talking about opportunities to help others is not to put a guilt trip on your kids but to educate them. Let them participate by helping at charity events, soup kitchens, giving to a family in need during the year or at Thanksgiving or Christmas. Over time your children will see firsthand how fortunate they are and will come to understand that life is not only about them or what whim they want fulfilled. It takes time, but talk about big topics in simple ways, without guilt, and show your children how you and they can help others. Explaining to them the way it fulfills you by helping others is heart-warming.

Meditation & Prayer

He who has faith has... an inward reservoir of courage, hope, confidence, calmness, and assuring trust that all will come out well- even though to the world it may appear to come out most badly.

B.C. Forbes

There are stories of ordinary people who have been put through extraordinary ordeals like Prisoners of War camps, Jewish families escaping a certain death, or a traveler lost at sea or in the wilderness for days. Each of them survived and talked about what kept them going and allowed them to get through the difficult ordeal, with some ordeals lasting for years. In each case the person spoke of Faith and love as being the overriding forces that helped to keep them sane and to maintain a will to survive. Faith is powerful. It gives us hope, courage and a sense of calm when we may otherwise find ourselves without any reason to have hope, to be courageous or to stay calm.

For most of us, when we speak of Faith we are using it to describe the Faith we have for our religious views, and this is the context in which I am speaking.

It is important to introduce our children to our own personal religious beliefs or those of our spouse.

You should be open about your beliefs with your children and practice your beliefs with your children.

I am a Christian, and my family and I pray and read scripture. We read children's bible stories before bed and attend church. Our children ask us many questions about our Faith and about God. We answer their questions with the best answers we can.

As your children get older, in their teen or young adult years, they may challenge the religious views with which they were raised. You should embrace their questions and desire to make sense of their own religious identity. Explain your beliefs to them, direct them to a respected religious elder or reliable books on the topic. The more open you are about your Faith and the reasons you believe, the more likely it is that your child will search and come back to a similar conclusion.

Teaching your children how to pray or even do meditation can have positive and lifelong benefits for them. There have been studies done that show how ill patients who pray have better outcomes and a more positive outlook on life. So spending time praying, learning scriptures or meditating can help your child not only have a relationship with God, but also help him/her learn to use prayer as a way to guide them, relieve stress, to find a calm inner place and to let go of the difficulties of the day.

Our Advice:

Share your beliefs and faith with your children.

Live your life to the best moral ability possible, giving your children a good moral example.

Answer questions about faith as truthfully as possible. If you don't know an answer, look up the information with your child.

Teach Kindness by Example

Ask yourself: Have you been kind today? Make kindness your daily modus operandi and change your world.

Annie Lennox

If you have children or grandchildren, it is important to begin teaching them about compassion and kindness and to show them by example. How the people around them treat others will determine the way they see the world and the value of people. For example, no matter where I am and who is assisting me, such as when I'm ordering food at a restaurant or fast food pick-up window, I thank the person helping me. I truly appreciate their effort and their attitude. But I know families who never thank those around them. If we show our children through our actions and words that all people are valued, no matter their job, their current life struggle, or their race or ethnicity, we will be teaching children a valuable lesson. Life is about loving all human beings, and everyone deserves to be treated with kindness and a loving heart.

OUT of THE BOX - FUN IDEAS

Creativity Box – fill a box with clay, pipe cleaners, foam shapes, markers, paints, brushes, scissors, glue, tape, construction paper, drawing paper, and colored pencils for spur of the moment creativity.

Recyclables Box – for building structures, animals and art sculptures. As you empty containers and small boxes, add these to your recycle box for using in creative activities.

DressUp Box – instead of packing the Halloween costumes and dressup outfits away for once-a-year use, keep them in a fun box or container for all-year use. Many fun accessories, such as Princess wands and Fireman hats, can be found at any dollar store across the country or from yard and garage sales.

Educational Fun Box – fill a box, or shelf, with inexpensive little workbooks containing educational activities, such as mazes, wordsearch, crosswords, and I Spy fun.

Magician Box- fill a box or bag with a few inexpensive magician things like a magic wand, playing cards, a bandana, then go online and print off a few simple instructions for learning magic tricks.

Shadow Puppet Box- put a few flashlights, paper, scissors, glue, crayons, and Popsicle sticks in a box. Let your kids make a few paper puppets, then let them shine the flashlights onto the wall in a dark room and use their puppets or fingers to make puppet shadows.

Mystery Box - go online to the family website www.ziggityzoom.com/fun and print a Case of the Missing _____ sheet. Fill in the sheet with your own clues and give it to your kids. You will have them trying to solve the mystery for hours to figure the mystery out. With the sheet give them a magnifying glass, pen and paper, and any other sleuth trinkets.

Inventor's Box - collect a few old boxes, containers, screws, nuts, bolts, yarn, and add glue, heavy duty tape, paint, markers, and paint brushes. Let your kids design and create an invention or creature out of the materials.

Budding Artist Kit - keep paints, small canvas panels (or heavy paper), crayons, scissors, and paint brushes in a box. When your kids need a creative activity pull out the art box.

Favorite Character Box- if you child loves a character from a storybook, the big screen, or just a special theme, fill a box with things you find related to that character, fabric scraps, stickers, dress up, decorations, anything.

Big Box – sometimes kids just need a big appliance box that has a few cut outs for doors and windows. It will keep them busy playing for hours.

Photographer Box- give your kids an old digital camera (or a kid-friendly or disposable digital camera) and head to a local landmark, park, or scenic place. Let them have fun capturing the activities of the day and sights from their perspective. It will keep their attention and give them pride in the pictures they took.

Nature Walk Box – grab some buckets or pails and go in search of neat nature treasures.

Surprise Box – each week, or month, put new things in a special box or bag and when you need a fun activity for your kids pull it out. (ex. stickers, pinecones, acorns, stampers, rocks, or anything sparkly).

FUN FAMILY IDEAS / ACTIVITIES

Indoor Snowball fight - use white socks balled up or white tissues, paper, or paper towels to make tons of indoor snowballs. Give each child and parent a container full of snowballs and have a ton of fun.

Plant a Garden

Put on a Play

Story Telling Time (campfire)

Roast Smores

Date Night w/ Each Child

Summer - Sharks & Minnows

Indoor Camping

Picnic

Candle Light Dinner

Geo-Caching

Treasure Hunt

Pin the Plane on the Globe (or map)

Stay-cation

Museum Day

Family Game Night

Dance

Travel Games

ONLINE ACTIVITY RESOURCES

ZiggityZoom.com – family website with fun and educational printables, craft ideas, online games and stories. Printable mazes, wordsearch, coloring pages, reward charts.

PBS Kids.com – kids website with printable activities featuring favorite television characters.

IN the CAR SANITY SAVERS

Printable Travel Games – there are tons of fun printables to be found online to use as travel games. Keep a folder of these in your car for use anytime the kids will be buckled in for a period of time.

Spur of the Moment Games – these are games you can play without any paper, pen or prop, such as :

- I Spy

- License Plate game

- Alphabet Spy game

PARENTING RESOURCES

WEBSITES

Diet & Behavior

www.drweigh.com

Special Education

National Center for Learning Disabilities

www.ncld.org

Internet Special Education Resources

www.iser.com

www.ldonline.org

Allergies / Food Allergies

www.AllAboutFoods.org

www.FoodFacts.com

www.FoodAllergyAssociation.org

Pediatrician Sites- Medical and Parenting Advice

American Academy of Pediatrics

www.aap.org

www.drgreene.com

www.askdrsears.com

ADD/ADHD

www.help4adhd.org

Autism, Aspergers/PDD

www.AutismSpeaks.org

www.AutismWeb.com

Anxiety and OCD

Dr. Tamar Chansky

www.freeingyourchild.com

Association for Comprehensive Neurotherapy

www.latitudes.org

International OCD Foundation

www.ocfoundation.org

Children and Adults with Attention Deficit/Hyperactivity Disorder

www.chadd.org

Anxiety Disorder Association of America

www.adaa.org

Sensory Processing Disorder Foundation

www.spdfoundation.net

Product Safety

Consumer Products Safety Commission

www.cpsc.gov

Environmental Health

Heavy Metals Analysis

www.Labbio.net

www.LabCorp.net

Educational Resources

www.school.familyeducation.com

www.nea.org/parents

www.education.com

Educational Printables

www.ZiggityZoom.com

www.tlsbooks.com

Healthy Eating Habits

www.FoodFacts.com

General Health

www.KidsHealth.org

www.cdc.gov

www.DrGreene.com

Emergency Information

www.cdc.gov

Building Self-Esteem

www.childdevelopmentinfo.com

Reading Readiness/Problems

www.ReadingRockets.com

www.dys-add.com/symptoms.html

Kids Technology/Media Safety

www.commonsensemedia.org

www.connectsafely.com

www.netsmartz.org

Family & Parenting

www.focusonthefamily.com

www.positiveparenting.com

Food/Product Recalls

www.fda.gov/Safety/Recalls

www.cpsc.gov

BOOKS

PREGNANCY

What to Expect When You're Expecting
by Heidi Murkoff

PEDIATRIC & MEDICAL

Raising Baby Green
by Alan Greene, M.D.

You: Raising Your Child: The Owner's Manual from Breath to First Grade
by Michael Roizen, Mehmet C Oz, and Michele Pawk

PARENTING

10 Days to a Less Distracted Child
by Jeffrey Bernstein, PhD

Grace Based Parenting
by Tim Kimmel and Max Lucado

How to Talk so Kids will Listen and Listen so Kids will Talk   by Adele Faber and Elaine Mazlish

Liking the Child You Love
by Jeffrey Berstein, PhD

Positive Pushing: How to Raise a Successful and Happy Child
by James Taylor, PhD

Raising Unselfish Children in a Self-Absorbed World by Jilly Rigby

Raising Your Spirited Child by Mary Sheedy Kurcinka

Scream Free Parenting: The Revoluntionary Approach to Raising Your Kids by Keeping Your Cool by Hal Edward Runkel

Siblings Without Rivalry: How to Help Your Children Live Together So You Can Live Too by Adele Faber and Elaine Mazlish

Stick Up for Yourself: Every Kid's Guide to Personal Power and Positive Self-Esteem by Gershen Kaufman, Lev Raphael & Pamela Espeland

The Happiest Toddler on the Block by Harvey Karp

NUTRITION & FOOD ALLERGIES

Feeding Baby Green by Alan Greene, M.D.

Little Sugar Addicts by Kathleen DesMaison

Red Light, Green Light, Eat Right: The Food Solution That Lets Kids Be Kids by Joanna Dolgoff, MD

Understanding & Managing Your Child's Food Allergies   by Scott H. Sicherer, MD

CHILDHOOD PSYCHOLOGY & BEHAVIOR

10 Days to a Less Defiant Child
by Jeffrey Bernstein, PhD

Parenting the Strong-Willed Child: The Clinically Proven Five-Week Program for Parents of Two-to-Six Year-Olds   by
Rex Forehand, PhD and Nicholas Long, PhD

The Defiant Child: A Parent's Guide to Oppositional Defiant Disorder
by Douglas Riley

What Your Explosive Child is Trying to Tell You
by Douglas Riley

CHILDHOOD NEUROLOGICAL

Parenting Children with ADHD: 10 Lessons That Medicine Cannot Teach
by Vincent J. Monastra, PhD

The Out-Of-Sync Child: Recognizing and Coping with Sensory Processing Disorder
by Carol Stock Kranowitz, M.A

About the Authors

Kristin Fitch is a parenting expert, speaker and the Editor of many family websites, including **ZiggityZoom.com** and **Mommie911.com**. She is the mother of three lively boys. Kristin regularly writes on parenting topics and speaks at parenting events, inspiring families to think outside of the box and expand their horizons.

Sharon Pierce McCullough has been involved in the parenting process of 17 children and grandchildren. She is co-creator of numerous family websites, including **ZiggityZoom.com** and **Mommie911.com**. An artist and designer, she is also the author of several "how-to" books and a Children's book series.